OJOMA'S *Melody*

BECOMING A LOVED WOMAN NIGERIAN STYLE

OJOMA EDEH HERR

Copyright © 2022 Ojoma Edeh Herr.

All rights reserved. No part of this book may be reproduced, stored, or transmitted by any means—whether auditory, graphic, mechanical, or electronic—without written permission of both publisher and author, except in the case of brief excerpts used in critical articles and reviews. Unauthorized reproduction of any part of this work is illegal and is punishable by law.

ISBN: 979-8-88640-589-7 (sc)
ISBN: 979-8-88640-590-3 (hc)
ISBN: 979-8-88640-591-0 (e)

Because of the dynamic nature of the Internet, any web addresses or links contained in this book may have changed since publication and may no longer be valid. The views expressed in this work are solely those of the author and do not necessarily reflect the views of the publisher, and the publisher hereby disclaims any responsibility for them.

One Galleria Blvd., Suite 1900, Metairie, LA 70001
1-888-421-2397

WHAT OTHERS ARE SAYING ABOUT OJOMA'S MELODY
BECOMING A LOVED WOMAN NIGERIAN STYLE

I met Dr. Ojoma Edeh Herr in June 2012, at a small church my family and I were attending. My first memory of her was when she walked into the church, marched up to one of the front pews, and then sang her heart out to the old hymns that were being played. I remember thinking, "Now that is a confident woman!"

Slowly but surely, we started to build our relationship. We started off as acquaintances, then friends, and eventually, mother and daughter. I have the privilege to call this confidant woman, Odumami. It means "my beloved mother" in her native tongue, Igala. My beautiful Odumami was born in Nigeria, and as you read her story prepare to be in awe with what she has overcome, but more importantly, how our Lord and Savior used her for His glory.

Her story will grip you from the moment you read the first page. Her perseverance, strength, intelligence, and faith will fill you with hope. While reading her story, you will undoubtedly see what our Lord can do through His willing vessels. For many years, I have personally witnessed her countless times in difficult situations where she completely relied on her faith in Christ, and He led the way. It is a beautiful site to behold. I pray that you see how good our God is, through "Ojoma's Melody" and are blessed by her story.

I love you Odumami. Thank you for being the example of Christ's love for me and others that have crossed your path. May the Lord continue to bless you on your walk with Him.

Your Daughter,

Stephanie Pizzulli (Omawe)

In 2020, it was my privilege to meet Dr. Ojoma Edeh Herr. She arrived from Nigeria on September 16, 1987. Hers was a journey filled with determination and tenacity. Ojoma's success as a professor at Millersville University is a testimony to the love and providence of God.

Ojoma's melody is a story of God's sovereignty and how He reigns and directs every aspect of her life. Her constant theme is that "Jesus Christ gets all the glory."

The reader will not be able to escape Ojoma's passion to help the oppressed and to love and serve others. She reminds the reader that all people are made in God's image and should be treated with dignity and respect despite their intellectual capacity. As she has reminded me often, "He has made all things beautiful in His time." I have learned this from personal interaction with her.

If you have not read Ojoma's Song, it would be to your advantage to read it as a prequel to Ojoma's Melody. Your compassion and love for the "least of these" will grow.

This current book will fill in the gaps of Ojoma's Song and bring the reader up to current events. What will the rest of her song like or how will her story end? Only God knows. How fitting that Ojoma means "God knows."

Reader beware: If Ojoma tells you she is praying for you, watch out! She has a direct line to her Father in Heaven.

Donna Fleming

A story of survival and perseverance... Very moving! Ojoma's testimony affirms God's mercy and grace as He promises his children a "Future and a Hope".

Gonny Gutierrez

From the office down the hall often emanates the music of another place and another's experiences. I have become accustomed to these sounds when Ojoma is working at her desk. During quiet times in our school day, Ojoma often sings to herself or hums along with her CD's. Are her tunes happy, sad, grateful, prayerful? I am never quite sure, but these songs have continued for the nine years Ojoma and I have worked together at the university.

In this tale of her days in Nigeria, Ojoma sings her song in a very simple and straightforward manner. She tells you about her own life experiences and the cultural expectations of her people as she grew into adulthood. Ojoma's story may appear foreign to the reader as she first sings it to you, but as each page is turned and you follow along as Ojoma simply sings you each verse of her life, you will soon come to recognize it as a very familiar tune. Ojoma's song is not unlike a comforting hymn that reminds both the listener and singer that, with faith, we are never alone and will ultimately overcome. This well -known song, Ojoma's story, is about the determination, purpose and faith of common people who, with God's help, deal with the personal adversities of life. Reading this story will open your eyes to the experiences of a woman in another culture. Ojoma's song reinforces the fact that faith will make the ultimate difference between a person merely surviving or overcoming and succeeding in her trials.

Cindy Ridley

CONTENTS

Dedication ix
Acknowledgement xi
Foreword xiii
Introduction xv

Part One
Patriarchal Oppression

Chapter 1   The Reconstruction of Events 3
Chapter 2   Welcome to the World of Men 7
Chapter 3   Beyond the Seven Days 10

Part Two
Hope and Determination

Chapter 4   My Education 17
Chapter 5   My So-Called "Marriage" 21
Chapter 6   Miraculous Love 28
Chapter 7   The Blessing of Detour 32

Part Three
Faith and Self-Actualization

Chapter 8   Welcome to the USA 39
Chapter 9   I am Truly Loved and Blessed 44
Chapter 10   By God's Grace Alone 49
Chapter 11   My skin color in the USA 54
Chapter 12   Mattaniah = Gift of Jehovah 58

DEDICATION

This book is dedicated to two beautiful women in my life. To my American mother, Mrs. Frances Martindale for her support of me when I came to the USA and my dear biological mother, Mrs. Omada Edeh, who was the pillar that held me up and who encouraged me to be all I can be.

ACKNOWLEDGEMENT

I would like to acknowledge the following people for their inspirations. Dr. Francine McNairy, president of Millersville University, for her inspiration, Dr. Cindy Ridley, the woman who understands and believes in me, Dr. Beverly Schneller, my encourager and the woman who brings the best in me out, Esther Anibe Edeh, my sister-in-law for her patience and naiveté's, Mrs. Frances Martindale (my American mother) for her support of me through tears and laughter, Mrs. Omada Edeh, my biological mother, for her unfailing love and encouragement. My mother was altogether lovely. I would also like to acknowledge my father, Edeh Egwu for his courage to show love to my mother and dividing his properties among his children, both males and females; Jonathan Herr, my son; Stephanie Pizzulli and Ajifa Aruwa, my blessed and miraculous daughters, and for my son Andrew Edeh Herr, his unplanned interruptions always showed me how much he loves me, Andrew is my constant reminder of how blessed I am to be a mother.

FOREWORD

Ojoma's Song is a celebration of God's Grace and an affirmation of His power in our lives. Simultaneously harrowing and hopeful, Ojoma's story is a joyful inspiration. Her accomplishments in an atmosphere of repression and oppression are a testament to her tenacity and unyielding faith in God's plan for her life.

Born in a rural area of twentieth century Nigeria, Ojoma possessed a vision of life's promise, available to her only as a true Christian. In a largely Muslim country, Ojoma's family embraced the Gospel and encouraged her to become educated and virtuous by living a Christian life. She overcame attempts on her life, mental and physical cruelty, and tremendous personal sorrows all in the name of her beliefs. She retained her drive to overcome and outlast, as well as outwit, her tormentors. Always a bit of rebel, Ojoma turned to God to guide her and preserve her no matter the obstacles.

Through the intervention of American missionaries, Ojoma was able to come to America as a young woman. The stories of her first days in this country, her confusion and her growth, are poignant. Not only did she apply herself to learning by first getting a GED, then an undergraduate degree, she also went on to earn her Ph.D. with Distinction from Columbia University's prestigious Teacher's College. She has now assumed a lively and productive career as a Professor of Special Education at a regional public university in Millersville, PA, where her duty is to train future teachers to work with special needs populations.

Ojoma Edeh Herr's generosity of spirit and heart are evident at all who know her. Her indomitable desire to see others reach their full potential runs through all her work. Perhaps because of the gifts of wisdom and perception that are innate in her character, Ojoma remains humble and unassuming. She is ever mindful of the Source of her gifts and of her successes – God and His Love.

Ojoma's Song captures your imagination. As a true story of a tumultuous life, you will laugh, cry and cheer Ojoma on and be deeply moved by every obstacle she surmounts. Her fascinating story will live in your heart.

Beverly Schneller

INTRODUCTION

> *The Lord is my light and my salvation*
> *Whom shall I fear?*
> *The Lord is the strength of my life*
> *Of whom shall I be afraid?*
> *Psalm 27:1*

As I sat in front of my computer crying and reading one more email making false accusations against me, my life flashed before me as if someone had put it in a single screen. What happened? Could I handle one more injustice? "Yes, you can" was the still voice inside reminding me of what I went through in my life to make me who I am today. I could not help but ask why; then, I remembered my promise never to ask God why. In fact, I did not want to ask, "why me?", rather, I wanted to ask God the what questions. "What do you want me to do God?" was what reminded me of the past and shaped my present and my future.

I kept the opening paragraph the same as the original publication. I wrote the original book after a few years of counseling, and this update is after a few years of a different type of counseling from an unexpected source and kept me continuously in the Word of God. As a result, I want to share the melody, most memorable aspect of my song with you.

Currently, I am a professor of Education at Millersville University. I am a blessed mother of four children: Ajifa, Stephanie, Jonathan, and Andrew. Thank you, Lord, for making it possible for me to experience the blessing of motherhood, which was one of my dreams as a young child.

I graduated with my PhD May 20, 1998, from Teachers College, Columbia University in New York City, ten years, and two days after I obtained my GED. Yes, GED. I came to the USA with only a sixth grade formal education in 1987, and eleven years later, I received my doctorate and started teaching at a university. The path I took was neither straight nor easy, but I made it by the grace of God. This is the message I want to communicate in this book. With God all things are possible. Originally, I shared my song, but this is a melody of how I became a loved woman in Nigeria and the journey I took to become the woman I am now.

PART ONE

PATRIARCHAL OPPRESSION

CHAPTER ONE

THE RECONSTRUCTION OF EVENTS

> *Before I formed you in the womb I knew you;*
> *Before you were born I sanctified you.*
> *Jeremiah 1:5*

As a child, I had two major dreams that were very important to me. In my mind, these dreams were inseparable. In setting out to pursue one dream, I believed that the second dream would be indirectly pursued. I was wrong! The Lord reminds me that my ways are not His ways as "He hath made everything beautiful in His time" (Ecclesiastes 3:11). My childhood dream was to provide education to as many children and women as possible. I envisioned that they could become productive members of the Nigerian society, of which I am/was a part, and marry a man who loved the Lord. As a child growing up in a poor family in one of the primitive villages in Nigeria, perhaps my dreams were fantasies rather than goals that could be attained.

Later in my life, my mother, father, sisters, aunts, uncles, and villagers told me pieces of my childhood story. Based on my understanding of my tribal culture, I have reconstructed what happened during my mother's pregnancy and the first years of my life. When my mother was "very old", either in her late forties or maybe even fifty years old, she became ill.

My mother had been sick for about two weeks and, not knowing that she was pregnant, she went to a local hospital which was six and half miles away to be treated. She complained about something that was moving in her belly. At that "old" age and having had many children already, she had not expected to be pregnant again, after my brother who had been born roughly three years earlier. (In my primitive village, we did not use birth certificates at the time my brother was born. Each family remembered when their children were born by the events that happen at the same time the children are born.). This hospital was known as a dispensary since the Nigerian hospital system is British-based. At the dispensary, the attendant told my mother that she was fine, but pregnant. She did not want to believe this doctor's diagnosis, but there was nothing she could do. The joke I heard many times since was that my mother, thinking that whatever was in her belly was a "sickness", asked the dispensary attendant if it was possible to have the sickness removed. The attendant said, "It will come out by itself in about five months." Immediately, my mother wanted to keep me and I am thankful about that! I am truly loved!

Other village women began gossiping about my mother, asking if she was really pregnant. My mother became troubled because of her age and worried about whether the baby would be healthy. While she was experiencing uncertainty and anxiety about my future, knowing me now, I can assume, I must have been praying to be born safely. After all, I had two dreams to fulfill! When the time came for me to be born, there was excitement in my country as a whole because I share my birth year with my country, though I could not wait to come on the actual Independence Day of October 1.

Let me provide a brief history lesson about the world into which I was born. Following the Napoleonic wars, the British expanded trade within the Nigerian interior. In 1885 British claims to a West African sphere of influence received international recognition and in the following year the Royal Niger Company was chartered under the leadership of Sir George Taubman Goldie. In 1900, the company's territory came under the control of the British Government, which moved to consolidate its hold over the area of modern Nigeria. On January 1, 1901 Nigeria became a British protectorate. In 1914, the area was formally united as the Colony and Protectorate of Nigeria. And on October 1, 1960, Nigeria gained her independence from the British. The irony of this is that I was being born in the year that Nigeria gained her independence and yet, as a woman, I did not have freedom in a male-dominated culture.

Like most babies of my time, I was born at home and delivered by a local midwife. July is one of the months in the rainy season, and I was born during one of the heavy rainstorms. Like many houses in the villages, my mother had a primitive mud house with a thatch roof and dust floor, so rainy seasons were usually and unusually challenging. In the primitive villages of Igala-land, husbands have separate houses from their wives. This makes sense because most men have multiple wives; however, even if a man has one wife, it is appropriate for the wife to have her own house separate from the husband. In most cases, when women are in labor, the husbands are the last to know, partially because they are in separate houses and partially because men were not supposed to have anything to do with the delivery of their children. This is not uncommon in other cultures, as I learned that at one time in the USA, husbands were not allowed in the delivery room either.

My mother was in labor, warmed by a wood fire, as she paced her tiny room which was about to be used for childbirth. In Igala culture, women in labor move around because they believe gravity will force the baby down more quickly. This is contrary to the Western practice where women in labor lay flat on their backs and are administered pain relievers as needed. My mother could not get a break; she was in pain and yet, she could not go outside to move around. At least, if it had not been raining, she could have paced in the backyard, but there was no such luck. It was raining very heavily. The roof was leaking, so that the rain dropped into the fire and made sizzling noises, which annoyed her. My mother was in pain and all sweaty and what I wanted was to come out! After all, I had two dreams to fulfill. I had a mission to accomplish; therefore, I must come…now! The children's noises from the other room aggravated my mother who was in serious pain. She was not crying, but she could not sit still. Labor and giving birth to a baby without any pain killers are things we lack words to describe. The Bible says, *"in pain you bring forth children" (Genesis 3:16a).*

It was time…time for me to be born. A friend of my mother's, whom I'll call Joy, was one of the local midwives and came to help her deliver. Joy told my mother to push. Have you ever wondered what babies think when their mothers are told to push? I can only imagine. Joy continued, "push, push, push…yes, you are doing well, push, push…I see the head… oh no, the head is gone back in…push harder…good, good, the head… the head is coming out…. GOOD! IT IS A…it is a girl. I thought it would be a boy", Joy announced with disappointment. If I could have spoken, I would have said something like, "oh my goodness! Joy can talk and she has the nerve not to like me because I am a girl." Fortunately, my mother said, "boy or girl, it does not matter. A healthy baby is all I want." My mother was a very special and a wise woman!

Joy continued, "It is only a girl, and she is no good. She is still breathing, but she will not make it." During that time in Igala culture, when the phrase "no good" was used for a newborn baby, it was a code which means that the baby was either premature or the baby has a noticeable deformity. This meant that the baby would not live long. In this case, I was referred to as "no good" because I was a tiny seven-month-old premature baby girl. Can you imagine how any child in my culture would feel to know that she is "only" a girl? Later, I saw other frail, premature babies delivered when I would go with my mother, who was also a local midwife, to deliver a baby. Thankfully, my mother refused to listen to anyone who told her that I was "no good". She took full care of me against Joy's advice. If I had not had a wonderful mother, I would have been left to die with minimal or no feeding at all. But my mother refused to listen to anyone; she fed me, cared for me, and kept me alive.

CHAPTER TWO

WELCOME TO THE WORLD OF MEN

And all of you are children of the Most High.
Psalm 82:6

It did not take me long to discover that I was born into a culture that values men over women. No wonder Joy had said that I was 'only a girl'. While this became a battle that I would fight for the rest of my life, I did not know it at that time. In my culture and during the time that I was born, when a child is born and the gender is announced as a girl, most men, especially in the villages would say, "my case is tomorrow." The phrase, "my case is tomorrow" is a patriarchal idiom implying that husbands can divorce their wives anytime they wanted for whatever reason. At that time, women were only good for one thing, to be married and have children, preferably male children. So, when husbands wanted to divorce their wives, they can; but women had no power/authority to initiate divorce from their husbands. Therefore, this phrase made sense to many men at that time period because the woman to be divorced would usually have no say. As a result, the only answer she would give her friends or anyone when asked "how is the situation between you and your husband?' is "my court case is tomorrow." Many village men have made a joke with this phrase that they use whenever a girl is born.

Of course, as a woman and a mother, such a phrase is not funny. No woman that I have asked has ever liked that joke, but it does not matter because women in my culture are truly in a world of men.

I learned quickly that I was born into a world governed by men. At this point, I can provide a list of men who consistently made my life miserable, or I can choose to emphasize the miraculous saving grace of God and I chose the latter. I am so thankful that "the Lord does not see as man sees, for man looks at the outward appearance, but LORD looks at the heart." (I Samuel 16:7). Everything I went through, both positive and negative as a child, young girl and young woman was all specially put in place by our heavenly Father for me before the creation and I can boldly say that I am loved!

Tribal marks were valued by my people at the time I was born. Some of these marks are beautiful and look like tattoos for lack of better words; while other types are just lines, with symbolic significances. Tribal marks were very important to many of the Nigerian cultures at that time because they serve as identification, a mark symbolizing belonging to a particular tribe. In addition to facial features, tribal marks also help combatants recognize "your own people during the tribal wars." Though my parents were not Christians when I was born; yet they did not give me any tribal marks. As I learned from my mother, I was too tiny when I was born and many people did not think I would survive; therefore, I was not given the tribal marks. As an adult, I am now very thankful that I did not get the tribal marks yet, as a child, I felt and still felt until five years ago, that I was not important or accepted by my people.

In the end, this lack of cultural identification gave me certain freedoms in my youth. Because I was no one, I thought I could subvert the sexual segregation my culture imposed. Specifically, my two dreams of education and equal love between husband and wife were contrary to the role of women as my society defined it at that time. However, I had two choices: to be compliant or to fight for equality. As a woman, I was trapped and my only option was to marry and have many children, preferably, boys. While I did not mind the having-the-children part of it, I did mind that

I must have children before I could be considered to have value! What happened to valuing a person because God values that person? I guess these are the questions that many people struggle to answer. While my struggle continues between me and my culture, I must first survive before I can fight for freedom.

CHAPTER THREE

BEYOND THE SEVEN DAYS

O Lord my God, in you I put my trust;
Save me from all those who persecute me;
And deliver me,
Lest they tear me like a lion,
Rending me in pieces,
while there is none to deliver.
Psalm 7:1-2

I survived my first seven days. Being born in a rainy season had its advantages and disadvantages. The obvious advantage was that I, as a premature newborn, did not have to go to the stream on my mother's back as she brought water home for use in the first month of my life. The major disadvantage was that, with the rain, the mud house with the thatch roof could leak or even fall at any time without warning.

My second week on earth was going very well; my mother could see that I was not losing weight. She was taking good care of her baby, and everything was fine until about the tenth day. On that day, the sky turned black, trees stood still, and the atmosphere was very quiet; a storm was about to begin, and it did rain very heavily. My mother said that I started to cry as if I was very scared of the rain. Looking back, I now have to ask, "was that heavy rain going to be a sign of how my life would be?" But of course, time would tell. It rained so heavily that the mud house with the thatch roof started to leak. Mother worried, "How can I keep this child dry and warm in this type of weather?" My mother talked to herself as she moved me from one part of the room to the other in hope of getting a dry spot for me and dry sleeping mats for six other children in her care. She found a dry spot for me, she thought, and she laid me down on the mat and went to attend to the rest of her children; and then I started to cry again.

Before my mother could get to me, the rain fell where I was laid on the mat and part of the roof caved in. My mother was afraid that the mud wall would fall, too. I was covered with part of the fallen thatch roof, but the wall was still standing. It was hard to believe, but I, the blessed child, survived the rain, roof caving and the frail mud wall that had miraculously stood firm. I am truly loved by God and by my parents. Overall, the first six months of my life proved challenging. I was sick often and my mother thought that I might not survive. At ten months, though still tiny, I took my first steps. Villagers were amazed and wondered how this "unfortunate child" could make such progress so fast. I did not gain as much weight as I should, but nevertheless, I appeared to be physically healthy. Praise the Lord!

By the age of five, another episode of serious "sickness" started in my life. It was very difficult for my mother because she hoped I would thrive when I did not die during my first six months of life. Nobody, not even my mother, however, knew of my pain, the suffering and the depression in my heart. Since I appeared healthy outwardly, everyone assumed that I was healthy inside as well. The scariest part of my new "sickness" was hearing people saying that I was possessed by evil spirits. I was not possessed. Here is the true story: I had been very depressed and injured in my spirit. My heart was broken and any determination I had to survive was fading. My people, my society and my culture could not help me, especially as I was a little girl and children are not supposed to have problems. For some reason, even as a little girl I was very saddened by how girls were treated by my culture…during the time I was born, my people did not believe that children should be heard. I was always punished by any adult who saw me for doing what the little boys were doing, climbing trees, pretend-hunting, cutting grass, "farming", etc. I was only supposed to pretend play how to cook, launder, and bring water and firewood home on my head.

I felt trapped with all these ideas and no way to express them. I think I was demoralized by the lack of a future for girls in my culture. My fear of being a girl trapped by my culture was so great that I thought I was going to be killed by men some day if I dared to break any rule. This fear turned out to be closer to reality than just a childhood fear. Many men, from some of my family to others in the village, had used the male power and put me in situations in which I was almost killed, but not at that time. I nurtured this thought of death so long as a child that it became a reality to me. I would hallucinate about three men dressed in white, from head to toe, carrying big swords and running after me, wanting to kill me. In response to the hallucination, I would run and cry out loud as I ran, "please, do not kill me." Whenever, my mother asked me what the problem was, I would tell her about the three men dressed in white robes running after me and wanting to kill me. My mother taught me phrases to use whenever I saw these three men coming after me. The phrases were, "Get behind me Satan; you have no place with me. I am a child of God." When these episodes of "sickness" happened many times, people concluded that I was possessed by evil spirits. During the time I was born, girls were not in demand in my culture and a girl who was possessed definitely was a disgrace to her family. Many people had different ideas about how to get rid of my "evil spirits" and one family member put this idea into action.

When I was about six years old, I was almost killed by a blood relative. This woman did not show my mother that she hated me; but the way she looked at me and talked to me when my mother was not around was an unpleasant indication of her feeling for me and my "evil spirits". Since my mother did not know her intentions, she was comfortable leaving me in her care whenever she offered to babysit for my mother. On this day, I had two episodes of the three men dressed in white chasing me. As I was recovering from them, a message came from my mother's father for my mother to come over immediately. I could not go with her because I was just beginning to recover from being "sick" and I was too big for my mother to carry me on her back for about a five-mile trip. As my mother was pondering what to do with me, this relative of mine, Laura, volunteered to take care of me. My mother, a wise woman, also asked a couple of our neighbors to keep their eyes on me while she was gone. This precaution ended up saving my life.

It was the driest season of the year; I do not know the exact month, but it must have been February or March. It was very hot and windy. The heat was bad enough that people could not stay indoors, even at night. There were no air conditioners or fans. Camping out came to mind since there was no electricity…and there still none for everyone in that village. Many people stayed under the trees to cool down during the day when these dusty, sandy Sahara winds blew. In spite of this intense heat, Laura put me into an old mud kitchen house on my father's compound. There was no window and only a little door to creep into the kitchen. She put a mat on the floor for me to lie on and then made a huge wood fire in the kitchen. The heat from the fire was enough to kill any living soul in that house. However, that was not enough for Laura. She began complaining that she was tired of me and my evil spirits and that she was going to cure me once and for all to put an end to this sickness.

I lay there helplessly. I could not say anything because I was afraid of her evil eyes looking at me. I did not know what I did wrong to bring this on. I cried silently as I wondered if I would ever see my mother again before dying in this hell that Laura had created. In Sunday school, our teacher had described what hell was like to us and now I thought I knew in reality. Then, Laura, added red hot peppers into this inferno. WOW! I considered this to be a punishment that should only be given to Satan; but I did not know what I did to deserve it. I started to think that *I must be really bad, as bad as Satan; otherwise, why should I go through this?* I closed my eyes when I saw my relative pouring the peppers into the fire. The peppers started to pop, entering my nose, eyes and throat making me to cough, sneeze, and cry very loudly. In a few minutes, one of the neighbors my mother had asked to keep an eye on me came and took me out. Laura told this neighbor that I poured the pepper in the fire myself and, since older people are always right and children are supposed to keep quiet in all situations, I did not say anything. My mother was told the same lie that I poured the red peppers in the fire, and I could not say anything in my defense.

A major fear in my adult life was that my mother would not know the truth about the fire story before she died. After two and a half years in counseling as an adult and in the USA, in the summer of 1992 I was ready to tell my mother the truth. Two and half months after I left my home that summer, my dear mother had completed her work on earth and went to be with our Lord and Savior, Jesus Christ on October 13, 1992. Laura may not remember what she did to me or maybe she is hoping that I do not remember. I will never forget it, but I have forgiven her, and I have vowed never to avenge myself using evil for evil. After all, she is a woman, and she has her pains as well. However, when adults take their angers out on children, it causes the abuse cycle to keep repeating itself and it never solves any problem. But sometimes, some women may not know what else to do and children pay for adults' mistakes. I am glad that God is with me and gave me the most wonderful mother. God gives me strength to handle life and not to give up. Praise the Lord!

PART TWO

HOPE AND DETERMINATION

CHAPTER FOUR

MY EDUCATION

To you, O Lord, I lift up my soul.
O my God, I trust in You;
Let me not be ashamed;
Let not my enemies triumph over me.
Psalm 25: 1-2

Many believe that my education was perhaps the most fascinating phenomenon in my life. God had His hands on me from the beginning. I believe that it is God's will that my dreams are fulfilled.

My education was one dream apparently not meant to be fulfilled if I had not been in God's care. But He made it possible, against all the odds, to bring His plans to fulfillment in my life. My people did not consider me to be a typical girl. I always liked to do what I enjoyed instead of what girls were supposed to do. Girls were supposed to be obedient, agree with everything men say, learn to manage a household, and be ready for marriage. I, on the other hand, loved to run, climb trees and be just wild. At nine, I was enrolled in primary school. Nigeria is the largest of the fifty-two African countries and runs what is called a 6-3-3-4 system of education corresponding to the years spent in the primary, junior secondary, senior secondary, and university, respectively. No girls of my age at that time went to school in my village, but I was enrolled in school because my mother wanted me to be educated. An added benefit was that the teacher was supposed to "beat some sense into me" as a student, so I could grow up and be a beautiful "obedient" young woman who was ready to get married. Well, as smart as I was as a young woman, I was not a strong student academically. I got into everything, meaning participating in boys' activities; therefore, creating many problems between me and teachers. I was caned frequently.

As there was no elementary (primary) school in my village; I was put in a school about 10 miles away from my village. I stayed with a family there, but I was supposed to come home every weekend and would go back to school on Sunday evenings. My mother and father would send me to school with plenty of food to last me till the next Friday, but the family I lived with would always eat my food; therefore, by Wednesday of every week my food was all gone. This happened faithfully every week. In my area, many villagers are very poor and some of them have difficulty feeding themselves and their children. Therefore, when I brought food from home, it was not an uncommon practice for the family to share the food that the girl staying with them brought. Culturally, this is not considered greed or stealing.

However, when I did not have food to last me for the week as my parents intended, it became problematic. So, I devised a plan. Whenever my food was finished and I was hungry, I would just go home. I thought it was a good plan, but my parents were very upset that I came home in the middle of the week. "Why did you leave school" they asked me. The first time I went home in the middle of the week, I told my parents the truth: "My food is finished, and I am hungry." But they did not really believe it. Not that they did not trust me but, they thought I was trying to get out of school for some reason. Afterall, as my parents' last born, I would want to remain in the village with them, they thought. They sent me back to school that Sunday with food for that week.

With my food finished once again, I had to come up with another plan. This time, I lied to my parents and said that I discussed with the people I was staying with that I was sick, and they told me that I could go home. My parents were very smart and knew that I was lying; but they said okay even though they did not believe my story. On the following

Sunday, my father wanted to follow me to verify my story, but I protested against it. Nevertheless, my father went with me to find out the truth. I was busted, but I had one more trick left; so I developed an even better plan, which I liked.

Since I was already in trouble with the teachers for participating in boys' activities, it made sense to me to team up with the boys. This time, I joined a group of boys and we started to steal small foods like bananas, oranges, etc. I was nervous at first since I had never done anything like that before. Each time we would steal, I was the only one caught stealing. The rest of them were "experts" and would disappear while I was left standing. One day, we stole bean cake in school, and I was caught, as usual. I was caned and whipped very badly by the schoolteachers. So, I decided that I have had enough of beating by the teachers, and I decided to get out of school; so I took off running. I was a very good runner. I ran and ran and ran. I was running towards home and I climbed one big tree and hid myself among the leaves. The teachers sent boys to pursue me and bring me back to school for more beatings. The boys that were running after me could not catch me I outran them, and hid myself so well that they could not find me.

I was so proud of myself because I was swifter than the boys. Looking back at that incident today, even though what I did was wrong, it was the first time I stood up to men and won. I hid myself in the tree until dark, and then I came out and spent a night in an abandoned house nearby. Before dark, I kept myself busy by going from one tree to another like a monkey, eating some fruits. My parents were told the following morning that I had disappeared. They were worried and came looking for me immediately. Soon afterward, I came out of my hiding place because I knew that my parents were worried about me. I loved my parents very much and I could not stand to see them worrying that much about me.

In situations like this one, many parents would have spanked their child, but my parents were different. My entire life, my father spanked me only once before this time that I remember, and my mother spanked me a couple times (each of which was done in love and to teach me a needed specific lesson which was beneficial to me). On this day, my parents were very scared that something had happened to me. Even though they were very disappointed with me for hiding in the trees and for putting my life in danger, spanking was the farthest thing from their minds at that time. Spanking in my country, at that time was not an abuse, and the type of spanking that my parents utilized with their children was done in love and for the purpose of correcting the child.

Troubles continued between me and the school. Though I socialized and played with a group of boys, no one touched me in any sexual way. We were innocent playmates. I think this also added to my confusion about why I could not do the things that boys did because I could not see any difference between us, other than the ways we dressed. I don't remember that anyone ever told me the difference between boys and girls; and I did not understand why I could not do the activities I liked, which happened to the same as the activities that boys did and were acceptable for them. Eventually, my parents changed my school. The change turned out to be the best move because at my new school I accepted the Lord Jesus as my Savior at the age of twelve and half years old. I never lied again, at least not that I know of, and I graduated from sixth grade in 1974, at the age of thirteen. I graduated in June, but soon afterward, my culture took over the direction of my life.

CHAPTER FIVE

MY SO-CALLED "MARRIAGE"

> *If that is the case, our God whom we serve is able*
> *to deliver us from the burning fiery furnace,*
> *and He will deliver us from your hand, O king.*
> Daniel 3:17

To follow the story of my so-called "marriage," you have to understand a little bit more about my world. During my youth, it was believed that the earlier a girl married the better. In my culture, the community functioned as a big family, which can be good, but can also be deadly if that community is the one to choose a husband for you. In my culture cousins, up to tenth generations removed, are considered to be close relatives and are usually referred to as "brothers" or "sisters." Any elder from your village or any relative from anywhere can bring you a husband. The husband to be is evaluated for appropriateness based on religion, lineage, and ability to feed his potential family. "LOVE" was non-existent in the evaluation. In a way, it is not too surprising because it is not possible for another person to determine anyone else's love. Now that you have a glimpse of this part of my culture when I was a little girl, here is my marital story.

Right before my fifteenth birthday, and after I finished my primary education, I went to work in a nearby dispensary opened years ago by Christian missionaries. This is the same dispensary that my mother had gone to about fifteen years earlier when she was pregnant with me.

Thinking about it now, I don't know whether there is any significance to this or not, but it sounds so weird that the same dispensary played two significant roles in my life. I first worked as an aide and later trained to deliver babies. My monthly salary was seven naira, about $7, now. I started working July 12, 1975, and I stayed with my cousin and his family who lived on the dispensary's compound which was on the hilltop and about half a mile from the town, his wife, and their two children. I was their house maid in exchange for room and board. Whatever money I earned was made available to me and my family.

My responsibilities in my cousin's house included doing everyone's laundry by hand, cooking for the whole family, doing dishes, cleaning up the big compound every morning, going to the stream three miles away, round trip, twice a day with eight to ten gallons of water on my head, bathing two children every night, going to the town's market to buy food, going to the grinding mill late every evening to grind cassava, corn, and other things that needed to be ground. To give you a frame of reference, cassava is the starchy tuberous root of a tropical African tree used as food such as tapioca. We use powdered cassava more often which requires lengthy processing. First, the root is dug up and the outer coverings are peeled. Then the peeled cassava is cleaned before soaking it in water for three days. I think the purpose of the soaking is to remove the chemical like taste from of the cassava. On the third day, the cassava is removed from the water and spread out in the sun to dry. When dried, the cassava is ground into powder before it can be used for food by adding the cassava powder into the boiling water. Corn, on the other hand, does not need to go through that process. When the corn is dried, the kernels are removed and ground into powder or soaked to soften it before it can be ground as liquid. My mistress had a business that required grinding corn in a liquid form, and this had to be done late in the evening.

On one particular night, I was coming from the grinding mill, climbing up the hill slowly with the load on my head, when I heard two men talking behind me. I was afraid and increased my pace, but they passed by me without saying anything to me. After I made it up the hill, a girl named Olive came to meet me with a message that her mother wanted to see me.

I panicked because Olive's parents were in charge of the dispensary where I was working, and I thought that I had done something wrong. When I asked my mistress' permission to let me go with Olive, she told me that she knew what the message was all about. "Clean your face a little bit," my mistress told me as I was covered with the white spots from the wet corn. White spots on my dark beautiful skin did not look attractive at all.

On our way to her house Olive told me that a man was there and he wanted to marry me. I was shocked, but did not say anything, but I reasoned with myself that "I am a woman and I have to obey everything whether it was right or wrong." Olive broke the silence by saying that I should be very happy because "the man is a customs officer." Well, I did not know what a customs officer was, so I did not say anything. I came to Olive's house and was led into Olive's room. An "old" man, whom I will refer to as Agatu, was sitting there waiting for me. (when you're fifteen, twenty-seven is old.)

"My name is Agatu," he said, "and your name is Mary right?" (Mary was the name that one of my parents' neighbors had given me when I was about eighteen months old. This neighbor became a Christian, had heard the name of Mary, and she wanted me to have that name.)

"Yes," I replied.

"I want to marry you. Can you come to my cousin's house tomorrow during the day? I want to see what you look like."

"Okay, but I have to get permission from my mistress first."

"I have to get you out of that situation soon."

"Okay," I said.

"Goodnight, Mary."

"Goodnight." I said bowing down.

The following morning, I went to Agatu's cousin's house where he was staying as he instructed me, but I covered my face the whole time I was there. I covered my face because I was very shy. On my way back to my place, I cried and cried, but could not do anything. I said to myself, "You are a woman now and you must behave like one." When the news reached my village, a family member took over and I was history. Before I knew it in five months, I was married to Agatu whom I had only seen once the first night and the second time the morning at his cousin's house with my face covered, all less than twenty minutes of introduction.

Back to my dream to be married, it turned out that I would get married, but not out of my free will or choice. My distant cousin, maybe ten times removed, brought this man into my life and before I knew it, a family member took over the whole process and I was to be married to Agatu. My parents did not say much because they let this family member take charge. The best I could hope for was to be one of the many wives. How could this be? How could I have considered myself to be married to a man when he was not really my chosen man? But I had to be obedient; that was what my culture expected of me. I did not want to marry Agatu, but I had no say in the matter.

Everyone was happy that I was marrying a customs officer with a high school education. But what I really wanted was to marry a local man, Joel, with whom I actually had fallen in love. Joel and his family lived about two and a half miles away from my village. But since he was not the choice of this family member, I had to obey the adults and be married to Agatu. I had wonderful parents, who were not appreciated by my people because they did not behave according to the cultural expectations. For example, my mother was the first woman in my area that started farming. My father loved my mother, and he was not afraid to show it. My father would allow me, a girl, to go hunting with him. Behaviors like these made people in the village look down on my parents, especially my father unfavorably. But this family member was expected to restore the name of my father to be cultural acceptability. So for my parents, when this family member said something, it was done and written in stone.

I did not sleep well a night before my wedding day. I managed to track down my wedding picture and this fifteen-year-old girl looked so sad in the picture. My night was a nightmare! I did not know that something like sexual relationships existed between a husband and a wife before I got married. For some reason, I did not learn or know anything about sextual activity, even during my wild years. My parents became Christians when I was about a year old, and I became a Christian at the age of twelve and half. The word "sex" was not in the language used by true Christians at that time, so I did not know what it was. Here I was, on my wedding night, required to be a woman, and I did not know what that meant. I managed to save myself from him the first night because all my family members that accompanied me were still there. The second night was HELL! I could not break myself from him and I had no idea what he was doing to me. The series of events that happened next are better left unsaid. In my opinion, some things are better left unspoken, and this is one of them. But I can tell you that the events were not pleasant!

I had to be taken to the hospital the next morning to get some stiches. It was in the hospital that a nurse told me what I was supposed to do as a married woman. When I was discharged from the hospital and came home, Agatu beat me severely because he reasoned that it was my fault that I was wounded and had to be hospitalized. To be fair, I was not the "typical" woman either. Remember even as a young child, I wanted to participate in activities that I liked instead of doing the "girlie" activities? Well, this time was no exception. I refused to accept everything Agatu said as the gospel. Therefore, I told him that it was not my fault and that it was his responsibility to teach me how to be a woman. Agatu's abuse started from that day on, and each time I disagreed with him, he would beat me up again.

A month after we were married he said I could not go to Church. However, I kept going to Church because I refused to let anybody stop me from worshipping God. At the age of twelve and half years old, I accepted Christ as my Lord and Savior. It was true conversion; I was not a social Christian like some people that were referred to as "church goers." So, when Agatu forbade me from going to fellowship with other believers, I had to disobey him and I continued to go to Church. This added fuel to Agatu's fire and increased the beatings and the kicking I received.

Three months after our marriage, Agatu planned to marry another wife because, according to him, I was barren. You have to know that women are like gardens. A garden that does not bring forth fruits or flowers is of no use to its owner. As the beating continued and I heard of his plans to marry another woman, I remembered what a doctor had told me when I was about fourteen years old. I told Agatu that a doctor had once told me that I would need to have a surgery before I could become pregnant. Reluctantly, he took me to the hospital. Sure enough, I needed to have a large ovarian cyst removed in order for me to get pregnant. Medically, I do not know whether cysts actually prevent some women from becoming pregnant, but that was what the doctor had told me.

About three months after my surgery, I became pregnant, but that did not change anything for Agatu, even though I was supposed to be on bed rest for the first five months of pregnancy. I went home to my family to deliver my baby, as it was the cultural practice at that time. I had the most beautiful baby miraculous girl. I was a week overdue, and I weighed forty-four kilograms when I delivered my baby. I labored for nineteen hours, with no pain killers, and when my baby came out, she was not breathing. My mother was in the delivery room with me and my midwife and had worked together before I got married. Both my mother and my midwife were praying and crying. I remembered the phrase kept saying over and over and over was, "Baby, please respond to your mother." Culturally, when a child is born and he or she cried, it means that the child responds to his or her mother. But as the Lord would have it, my baby started to cry and she was and still is beautiful.

Though I had a baby, yet that was not good enough to stop Agatu's abuse, especially since my baby was not a boy. At this point, Agatu was tired of my "disobedience", of going to church when he forbade me from going. He wanted to divorce me, but the church elders of my Plymouth Brethren denomination refused to let me leave him, stating that "marriage is for life". I was stuck! I had nowhere to go as I envisioned the walls around me coming together very quickly and I thought the only way out was the divorce; but I was wrong. The only way out was to look up to the Lord and He would airlift me. "Oh! It is horrible to be a woman" I said to myself. But I had to look up and believe that the Lord would always be faithful to His words. Though the situation seemed very hopeless; I knew that the Lord would never let go of me even when I could not hold on to Him anymore.

My pains in Agatu's house continued when I was poisoned twice. Poison is one of the many ways an enemy can be destroyed by witch doctors in my culture. I was poisoned; but did not know for sure who poisoned me. The first poisoning happened while I was still with Agatu and the second one occurred when I was fighting against his divorce. I do not know how the poisons were done, but I do know that they are very painful. When I was in pain for the first poisoning, my right leg was almost cut off. Something was moving under my flesh and would station itself from joint to joint. The poison would go from one joint to another, and the pain could not be explained by any words. I went to the hospital against Agatu's will. The specialists that examined me could not find any medical reason for my pain and suggested that my right leg could be cut off as the poison had stationed at my right knee for more than a week. But the Lord was good yesterday, He is good today, and He will be good tomorrow, praise His precious name! My leg was not cut off. Shortly after this, I was hospitalized by the last beating I received from Agatu and when I was released from the hospital, he was advised to take me home to my parents before he killed me. He did. Perhaps, that was the only good thing he had ever done for me, taking me home to my village and to my family.

With the second poisoning, my joints were not frozen as in the first one, but my ankles were swollen with serious pain. When my ankles were slightly cut in an attempt to let the native medicine herbs, into my body to cure me; the blood that flowed was as black as charcoal. Through all these trials, I miraculously survived. The Lord is greater than all evil forces!

After my marriage to Agatu was over, I went to a Bible School in a nearby town to study the Bible. I really wanted to go there because I wanted to know the type of sins that I had committed to make life so difficult for me. "Why was my life so bad?" I wanted to know. I wanted to find out from the Bible for myself instead of by men, especially a family member's interpretations of it. Well, I ended up going to that school for three years and I learned and learned that the major sin I had committed was being born a girl. The struggle continued. If my major sin was being a woman; then I needed education. In my culture as a woman, and worse yet, as "a divorced woman", there was no future for me without education. But as a "divorced" poor woman, I had no way of getting education. The next phase of my struggles began.

CHAPTER SIX

MIRACULOUS LOVE

> *My heart rejoices in the LORD;*
> *My horn is exalted in the LORD.*
> *I smile at my enemies,*
> *Because I rejoice in Your salvation.*
> *No one is holy like the LORD,*
> *For there is none besides You,*
> *Nor is there any rock like our God.*
> *1 Samuel 2: 1-2*

Chapter six of the first publication of this book was titled "Lost Love." That chapter chronicled my devastating journey when my beloved daughter, Ajifa was taken away from me at the age of five days before she turned three years old. As a result, I did not know where she was, and she did not know me. The opening Scripture passage I used was:

> *I am troubled, I am bowed down greatly;*
> *I go mourning all the day long.*
> *For my loins are full of inflammation,*
> *And there is no soundness in my flesh.*
> *I am feeble and severely broken;*
> *I groan because of the turmoil of my heart.*
> *Psalm 38:6-8*

Instead of chronicling the thorns on the rose bushes that paved the paths I have taken to be where I am today, I chose to focus on the beautiful roses on my journey. I am truly loved by God, and I want to share some of these miracles to encourage you.

I had prayed to have a baby girl so that I could braid her hair and dress her up beautifully, etc. The little that my teenage mind knew about babies, I loved the idea of a baby girl. I was blessed with a baby girl. It is so easy to overlook this answered prayer of having a baby girl. When my baby was taken away from me, five days before she turned three years old, I prayed that God may keep her alive and reunite us some day. In her struggles without her mother, God protected her, and my baby survived, which was another answer to prayers. And though the reunion did not go as I had prayed, I did get to see her again when she was a teenager, ten years after she was taken from me.

Chapter ten of the first publication of this book was titled "Where is She?" That chapter chronicle the ups and downs of my journey before I was finally able to see my daughter. But I chose to focus on the miracles on that journey. The opening Scripture passage I used was:

Blessed are those who mourn,
For they shall be comforted.
Matthew 5: 4

Before I left Nigeria in 1987, there was no sign or hope of seeing my daughter. The year 1988 was an unforgettable year for me. Not only did I come to live with my newly adopted American mother, I got my baby's direct address, which meant that I could write to her. In addition, I got my GED, May of 1988. I finally had a High School Diploma! With God, all things are possible.

In February 1989, I received this beautiful letter in the mail which read, "Dear Mum, I am glad to know where you are at last..." I kept writing many letters, sending pictures to her. My biological brother was in school near where my daughter was, and he decided to go and see her. I truly appreciate him doing that for me. He made two unsuccessful trips to her mailing address in an effort to see her. Finally, he was able to see her on his third trip.

In April, 1989, I received another letter in the mail which said, "Mother, please come home this year so that I may know you for the first time in my life. Are you older than my uncle that came to see me or younger? Are you fat or slender? Are you old or young? Are beautiful or ugly?", etc. She had many personal questions to ask about me since she could not picture how her biological mother looked in her mind. The same solid wall that was built around her to prevent me from seeing her did not have any magic mirror for her to see me on her side and nobody talked about me to her.

In the summer of 1990, I was able to go home to see my baby, risking not been able to return to USA since I did not have a return visa. By July 1990, I was able to see my baby; the exact month that she was taken away from me ten years earlier. What a big and most blessed birthday present! My birthday is July 14, and I waited ten years to get this wonderful present that I almost did not think possible. My visit with her was very brief as I promised the matron not to interfere with her school schedule. Since then, I decided to go home every year to see my baby, who said to me on the last visit before she graduated from high school, "Mum, I am not a baby any more; I am a woman now." She may not be a baby any more, but she will always be my beautiful baby girl. My mother was right. God does make a way where we think there is no way. One doesn't need to lose hope. One must hold firm to the faith and trying not to sing the "poor me" songs.

Did I return to USA that summer? The miraculous event surrounding my return to the USA is hard to believe. In fact, I did not believe it at first. I thought it was a dream, but I looked at the stamps in my Passport and I realized that it was truly a miracle. I applied for the USA visa to return, and my visa application was denied. In 1990, one has to wait three months before reapplying if the visa was denied. As I was coming out with a missionary who applied and got a visa for her daughter, one of the USA embassy gate workers approached us as asked, "Did you get your visas?" The missionary said yes, and I said no. This man told us to go back in and have the missionary confirm my story to the officers inside. This makes sense since the USA citizens go in through a different door than noncitizens. We did as the man said and my visa application was approved in less than two hours after it was denied, and I was to come back the next day to pick it up. When we came out, I wanted to thank the man, but he had left, so I thought that his shift had ended. The next day, I came to his gate to thank him, but he was not working that day. After I got my visa, I went and boarded public transportation, like buses station, to go to the village. To my surprise, the same man was smiling and waving goodbye to me, having water on his head and sell to the travelers. I was half waving, with a shocking look on my face. I must admit that his smile was very comforting, but I questioned how a man with a prestigious job be happily selling water, which was the lowest job? Did God send me an angel? It took me long time to share this experience with anyone and I have my stamped Passport as a witness. Not only was I able to come and see my baby, but against all odds, I got visa and returned to USA.

The above were not the only miracles in my life. But those were listed to give you a window to see why I am who I am today. Sometimes, it is easy to miss what God has called us to do. My calling is "Saved to serve." There were many opportunities on my journey that could have caused my death, yet I am still alive today. Why?

God saved me to serve Him and others. When I was in Jos, during my so-called "marriage", I was miraculously saved, again. Wives, young and old, go to the local markets to buy groceries and I did. On my way back, with other women, we encountered storm, heavy rain, and wind. In short amount of time, the roads flooded with rapid, powerful gushing of water on the roads. Before we could figure out how to get out of the road to safety, we were swept away by the flood. We were screaming for help, but help did not come to us in time. What felt like ten miles in this situation, the violence wave threw me up and smashed me against some rocks formation and I was wedged there. The storm lessened and I was rescued and taken to the nearby hospital. Thinking the other women on the same road with me were in the same hospital, I asked how they were doing. It was then I was told that many of them perished. Why was I saved?

CHAPTER SEVEN

THE BLESSING OF DETOUR

> *But seek first the kingdom of God and His righteousness,*
> *and all these things shall be added to you.*
> *Therefore do not worry about tomorrow,*
> *for tomorrow will worry about its own things.*
> *Sufficient for the day is its own trouble.*
> *Matthew 6: 33-34*

Chapter seven of the first publication of this book was titled "A Detour to Exile." That chapter yet chronicled why I ended up in exile and what happed to me during the thirteen months journey while there. The opening Scripture passage I used was:

> *My loved ones and my friends stand*
> *Aloof from my plague,*
> *And my kinsmen stand afar off.*
> *Those also who seek my life lay snares for me;*
> *Those who seek my hurt speak of destruction,*
> *And plan deception all the day long.*
> *Psalm 38: 11-12*

Traditionally, I do a family devotion every evening before my boys go to bed. We read through the Bible, in addition to them reading their children Bible every evening. For some unknown reason to me, in 2013

I decided that my boys and I would read Proverbs monthly for the entire year. The book of Proverbs is full of wisdoms and a practical guide for Christian walk. Though my boys did not know why we focused on one book of the Bible for a year, they were happy. During that year, I prayed continuously that God may reveal to me who He wants me to be, and He did!

Many positive and negative things were happening in my life, but I chose to focus on the lesson the Lord wanted me to learn from them. I was still broken about not having my daughter in my life, even though I brought her to the USA. I would say these words to myself, "I am not getting counseling. I am tired of it." Sometimes I wonder what the Lord say the moment I begin one of my self-pity parties. Ojoma! Yes, that is my name and my name Ojoma means, God knows.

Ojoma, indeed! In 2014, what seemed to be out of nowhere, I was contacted by a wonderful woman who worked for one of the major newspapers in Lancaster County, asking my views on the kidnapping of young girls in my country, Nigeria. This woman then asked me if I would be interested in writing a column for the paper's "Matter of Faith" section. I said yes and the Lord used this to provide me with the counseling that reminded me that I am a loved woman. So, I said goodbye to my self-pity parties and said, "Here am I!" (Isaiah 6:8b) saved to serve.

I am going to share two of the faith columns I wrote with you.

A worrier enters the new year with trust in God (published by LNP January 4, 2015)

The celebration is over and now each of us is left wondering what the new year may bring. Is my job secure? Is the economy stable? Is the housing market picking up? Can I pay my bills? Can I feed my family?

These and many other questions flood our minds as we think about the new year. It is easy to worry about the future, and many of us do. The great British thinker C.S. Lewis, one of my favorite authors, wrote: "The next moment is as much beyond our grasp, and as much in God's care, as that a hundred years away.... In neither can we do anything, in both God is doing everything."

As a worrier, I truly appreciate this quote because I know that I cannot change one thing that I worry about but having faith in God changes everything. Matthew 6: 25-34 clearly spelled this out for me. "Which of you by worrying can add one cubit to his stature?" This is what the C.S. Lewis quote above was referring to, and of course none of us can answer this question with "I can." This means that we should not be anxious, or become distressed and perplexed as we face the future.

Since no one can predict the future and we are not supposed to worry about it, what can we do?

Elvis Presley sang a song titled "Tomorrow Never Comes." But that was just a song. We know that tomorrow flows into today and will do so until the end of time. The future has always been and always will continue its unending approach. My name Ojoma means "God knows", and God truly knows the beginning from the end. He is our past, our present, and our future; therefore, we need to trust our unknown future to a known God.

Though I don't remember where I heard the quote, "I don't know what tomorrow holds, but I know who holds tomorrow", I know that it applies to those of us who are worriers. It does not matter that we are not able to see the future, but it is important that we have faith in God who knows our future. We know that neither fear nor doubt can change anything, but having faith in God changes everything.

The future is fascinating and may at times even be terrifying. The future will arrive without consideration of needs and we have no way of controlling it, but God does. God has plans for our today, He has plans for our tomorrow, and He has plans for our future. God clearly revealed His plans for us in Jeremiah 29:11, "I know the plans I have for you, plans to prosper you and not to harm you, plans to give you hope and a future." Why then give way to worrying as to how we shall meet the future necessities? God values us more than the birds of the air that He feeds every day, and more than the flowers of the field He clothes in beauty.

As a worrier, I can now say that if God says it, I will believe it and if God promises it, I will claim it. Therefore, let all of us claim God's promises with confidence and hand over our next moment, our tomorrow, our year, and our future to God who knows and can do everything.

The God who clothes the grass of the field has promised to clothe us. Happy New Year!

Lesson of Integrity, wisdom in Challenger explosion (published by LNP January 31, 2016)

The words that permeate my thinking lately are integrity and wisdom, and how both can be compromised by personal loyalty. James 1:5 states, "If any of you lacks wisdom, let him ask of God, who gives to all liberally and without reproach and it will be given to him." This easy-to-understand verse is very difficult to practice in real life.

I have been reflecting on the space shuttle Challenger disaster, one of the profound events that changed the history of this great nation. January 28, 1986, thirty years ago, was a cold day at the launch site in Cape Canaveral in Florida. Some distance away and unknown to the nation, a war of words raged behind the scenes between clear-thinking engineers who said, "No" to the launch, and executives and image-conscious individuals with authority who said, "Yes."

Seventy-three seconds after launch, the Challenger's crew of seven perished.

The real reason, in my opinion, for the demise of Challenger is the breakdown of integrity, both in the construction of the shuttle's solid rocket boosters and in the character of those who refused to heed the warnings. Similarly, there is a breakdown of integrity among people of faith today due to misguided loyalty or image consciousness. As stated in Proverbs 20:7, "The righteous man walks in his integrity, his children are blessed after him."

Merriam-Webster partially defines integrity as "an unimpaired condition…, the quality or state of being complete or undivided." When one has integrity there is an absence of hypocrisy. He or she is personally reliable, privately clean, and innocent of impure motives. Integrity is not only the way one thinks, but the way one acts. It evidences itself in ethical soundness, intellectual veracity, and moral excellence. It is honesty at all cost, and is rock-solid character that won't crack when standing alone or crumble when pressure mounts.

Having integrity won't always win friends. As in the Prophet Daniel's case, others will often turn up the heat on those who display integrity (Daniel 6:5). Just as Daniel did not compromise his integrity under pressure, we people of faith need to resist giving in to pressure and compromising our integrity.

In addition to having integrity, God wants us to possess wisdom that comes directly from Him. The Bible says that wisdom is more valuable than rubies and gold. Webster's defines wisdom as "the natural ability to understand things that most other people cannot understand, knowledge of what is proper or reasonable: good sense or judgment."

Today, our world seems to be filled more with "wise guys" than wise people. Wisdom changes what we do, as well as who we are. Wisdom is more than knowledge. Wisdom knows what to do with knowledge; it is something that enables us to see what is right and to do it.

The engineers and technicians who said, "No" to launching Challenger and Daniel who said, "No" to worshipping the king's image are people of integrity and are wise. Spiritual wisdom is a gift from God, and God gives it to whoever cares enough to ask. Ask for wisdom today and ask again tomorrow and the next day.

The Challenger crew's lives, and sacrifice are not forgotten. The impact is as profound today as it was thirty years ago.

Our God is an awesome God! He provided me with opportunity to do what I like to do, which is writing, and that assignment led me to study the word of God in depth so that I can let of go of my worrying. I am saved to serve!

PART THREE

FAITH AND SELF-ACTUALIZATION

CHAPTER EIGHT

WELCOME TO THE USA

> *Who remembered us in our lowly state,*
> *And rescued us from our enemies,*
> *Who gives food to all flesh,*
> *Oh, give thanks to the God of heaven!*
> *For His mercy endures forever.*
> *Psalm 136: 23-26*

I just want to say a little bit about my experience in America, my ups and downs and how I became the person I am today. I am very thankful to God Almighty who made it possible for me to be in this land of opportunities where I have come to enjoy all the benefits of God's plan for me. On September 16, 1987, at about 5pm, the Air Italia plane landed at JFK Airport. I have to say that before my trip to America, I had never seen an airplane so close. Flying from Nigeria to Rome and then from Rome to the United States was quite a trip for me. I realized when I came to America, that the country was full of excitements and confusion. The cultural shock was overwhelming for me, and I had much to learn about becoming the kind of woman valued in America.

The first culture shock I experienced was coming out of the airport where friends and relatives met the arriving loved ones. I saw a man and a woman hugging and kissing each other in public. The hugs weren't really that bad since we hug one another at home as well; but a man and a woman kissing in public? I was not ready to see that yet. In addition to that, they were holding hands. Mind you, it was only shocking because it was done in public. I had never seen anything like that done in the public before that day.

The person who came to meet us at the airport took us out to eat. I had never seen so many different types of food in my life! There were so many choices that I was literally paralyzed and could not make a choice. The place we went to eat was one of the cafes in which you serve yourself. I just took a bowl of green lettuce. The missionary that I came with said, "Mary, take more food. Salad is like a side dish here. Take more food." I said, "Oh no; this is good enough, thank you"; not knowing what else to say. I was not full; I was just paralyzed with so many foods to choose from that I did not know what to take. There were so many different types of food; I just could not pick one.

I ate my "salad" and we left for New Jersey. Another experience that was shocking since we were about to land, and continued everywhere I went that evening, was the many lights, different colors of lights. Coming from a village where there is no electricity it was a little scary to be honest. Not scary in the sense that something bad was going to happen to me, but I was shocked. Finally, we came to the mission station where we were supposed to stay for two weeks. I was relieved, because the two-bedroom apartment for the three of us, the missionary, the girl with disabilities I came to care for and me, was small enough to "close out" the outside world. When we closed the corridor door, I was so happy because we locked many people out. At least, I was with the people I knew.

Do you want to know what happened? We all took showers. Though I was trying to get used to taking showers, the first night I took a bath since that was what I was used to. What a difference a few years make! Today, I prefer showers to taking a bath. Talk about cultural differences! I finished my bath, and everybody was ready for bed. I was so tired with the time change. We gained five hours coming here so when we came to our destination it was actually 2 o'clock in the morning the next day where I came from. I was so tired at this point, my head hardly hit the pillow when I fell asleep.

Can anyone get a culture shock in his or her sleep? Well, I did. I had just fallen asleep when a loud noise woke me up. I panicked, terrified, and shaking because I had not slept for long when the noise woke me up. I went to the missionary and asked, "What was that?" She said, "Oh that is the telephone. The person that brought us was just checking to make sure that everything was fine." "Telephone?" I asked, while still shaking with the loud noise that woke me up. Mind you that the village where I came from, was so peaceful and the only noises you hear are the nature noises, not man made noises. At that time, in my village, no one had a car and just one or two people had motorcycles. Some people had bicycles which they traveled with so it was really peaceful.

Suddenly I felt like a fish out of water. Not only a fish out of water, but a fish picked up from the Pacific Ocean and just dropped in the Sahara desert. I didn't know what to do. Everything was so different here. The fear I experienced was so different and so strange that I just could not explain it in words.

I brought some resentment with me when I came to this country. But it all vanished the first night. I used to think that all white people living in USA took my people for slaves. I was very upset as I knew West African history well enough to know about the slave trade. What I thought I was supposed to do if I ever came to America was to fight against the injustice of the slavery. The man that met us at the airport was white and most people we visited the first few months of our arrival to USA are white as well. All these people treated me so nicely and respectfully that it was different from what I was expecting from all white people. I thought all white people were mean and discriminatory; but I realized quickly that I was wrong. The slave trade was ended years ago, and the people here today are the grandchildren or the great grandchildren of the people that had done this devilish act. So, the white people here today might be just as upset and angry with their great grandparents' behavior as I was with them. Why punish the children for the sins of their ancestors? Mind you, there is still discrimination in America today. But what I am saying is before I came here, I thought every white person in America discriminated and used black people as slaves. I was wrong, it was not like that. I discovered and learned all these things on my first day in America. That was a pretty good lesson, don't you think?

My second day in America was full of many fresh culture shocks. I did not think anything would surpass my experience on day one. But that was because I did not know what I was getting into in my day one in America. So, day two even though I didn't know everything I was going to see, I knew it had to be different. I am not going to go through my day-by-day life experiences in America, though I know that each day is as important as the other. I am just going to explain what everybody has taken for granted here in America. When I hear a lot of people complaining here, I always want to tell them to count their blessings. If only they could see what is going on in my country, or in my continent; they would appreciate what they have.

Day two began with eating breakfast cereal. I think it was raisin bran; but there was nothing really shocking about that. However, I could not find milk when the missionary asked me to get milk in the refrigerator. I said, "I can't find milk." She came and picked up a small box and she told me, "This is the milk." I could have read the label, but I was expecting to see the powered milk we use at home. Later on I said, "I wish I really had had somebody to educate me about what America was really like before I came here on my first day." I wished there were some people to tell me what to expect instead of my learning by trial and error. But I quickly realized that learning by trial and error is actually a better way to learn to master some things. I have learned not to take anything for granted. Not to take people for granted, not to take anything I see for granted, but to be thankful, appreciative and inquisitive about them all. The missionary opened the milk and I was looking at how she opened it so that the next time I would not have to be ignorant about that. I could not eat breakfast because the milk was too cold and I was not used to eating cold stuff like that. (Some things never changed, I still do not like cold stuff.). I went back to the refrigerator and took the milk out and looked to see why one side could be opened and the other could not. Then I saw the arrow and I said, "Good" to myself.

That evening, before the missionary cooked, she said to me, "we are going to have chicken tonight." I said "okay." However, inside, I was thinking, *How can we have chicken tonight? You don't eat chicken as a meal; you eat yams, potatoes, pounded yam, rice, beans and all those things. How can you eat chicken tonight?* To us, we use a little bit of meat or smoked fish, if you have it, to flavor the food. So we don't eat meat for dinner. We use it to give taste to the food. But to my surprise, she cooked chicken and rice and gave me a whole half of a chicken breast. I was horrified! How can I eat so much meat? I did not even eat half of it and I was tired of eating the meat. I was even more surprised when everything was thrown away. I was shocked and horrified and I went to the bathroom and cried. "Oh my goodness, how much food do people waste in this country? Don't they know that people, somewhere else, are hungry and have little to eat? Why do they waste so much? Why did she give me half of a chicken breast to begin with? I still have the same question today as I did years ago, but now I can almost finish half of a chicken breast. Yes, there is a waste here, but who am I to complain? I went back to the Bible to comfort myself. God gives according to His Divine plans and purposes, and I do not know those plans and purposes. Who am I to question what God does? The experience continues.

I am very thankful that the Lord brought me to the USA, the land of many opportunities to realize my childhood dreams.

CHAPTER NINE

I AM TRULY LOVED AND BLESSED

> *Blessed are the merciful,*
> *For they shall obtain mercy.*
> *Blessed are the pure in heart,*
> *For they shall see God.*
> *Blessed are the peacemakers,*
> *For they shall be called sons of God.*
> *Matthew 5: 7-9*

Chapter nine of the first publication of this book was titled "2732 Hillview Road." The address was my adopted American mother's address when I came to the USA and I stayed with her. In the original chapter, I chronicled my experiences while I lived with her and those experiences were beautiful and meaningful. For this updated chapter, I want to shared how blessed I am to have her as a mother and to honor all my friends by sharing one faith column. I am keeping the same opening Scripture passage I used to honor both groups.

Well, I must talk a little bit about my American mother, Fran, whom I lived with for five years. She fell in love with me and I fell in love with her. She had a mother who went to be with the Lord in May of 1990 at the age of 96. But when she was alive, I called her "Grandma." She used to call me any name that came to her at the time. She was getting old and she was getting our names mixed up. She was so sweet. She used to scold her daughter, Fran, for my sake. She thought her daughter was not taking good care of me. Even though I was an adult, Grandma would give me her food because, according to her, I never had enough to eat. She loved my singing too, even though I do not sing well. I would sing to her and she would throw both her hands up while enjoying the song immensely. The last Easter that I spent with her before she went to heaven was Easter of 1990. Her daughter, Fran, and my adopted mother, came to her and said, "Mother, Jesus is alive! He rose from the dead." Grandma said, "O-o-ooh, who told you?" I was standing right there, and Fran said, "Peter, Andrew, John, Mary Magdalene and all the disciples." Grandmother said, "Won't the Father be glad!" It was so precious; you would have had to be there to see how precious it was. My grandma was a woman of faith, and I can write a whole book about her.

I do not think that it is possible for any mother to love her daughter more than my adopted mother loves me. Even though I came to USA as "an adult", I desperately needed a mother and God provided me with the best one. We had many fun memories together and we shared some tears as well. My adopted mother and I can share many funny, wonderful stories about hot dogs, hair, Becky's legs, Okra, Happy New Year, Cauliflower, to name but a few. We were good for each other, and I miss her every day. She completed her work on earth and went to be with the Lord January of 2013. When I came there, I remember saying to myself that dust must not be able to penetrate her house. I had never seen a house so clean. It turned out that dust did come in; she just kept everything so clean all the time that you could not see any dust. What a challenge for her to have someone like me in the house. My room was always full of papers from schoolwork and my bed was very rarely made. When I left for school, she would come into my bedroom and make my bed and picked up all the papers. At first, I did not say anything, but when I became comfortable with her, I told her not to clean my room anymore. Yes, you can say that I was spoiled by my mother. One day, she found a cartoon in a newspaper and cut it out for me. In the cartoon, a little boy's room looks like a tornado has just landed there and his friend was saying, "I like what you've done with your room." Well, we both laughed until she was blue in the face, and I was purple.

This story is funny knowing that my adopted mother is a *very* proper lady. My nickname for her was "Queen Elizabeth" and she is that proper and elegant. Since the cartoon, I started to keep my room semi cleaned. We had fun with that one.

I must admit that I am the most blessed woman on the planet earth. Yes, I did not have it easy, but I have had two great mothers, both loving me immensely. More importantly, both of my mothers love the Lord with all their hearts. My adopted mother would never say anything that she was not sure of. I told many of my friends that a couple of my adopted mother's favorite phrases of were: "Let's pray about it for the Lord to reveal it to us. Let me think and ponder about it first, after all, the Lord is in control." What a woman of faith. The one other person I knew who exhibited her qualities was my biological mother. Yes, Mrs. Frances Martindale was my adopted mother and she was married for the first time at the age of seventy-eight. Did I mention that she was courageous, wonderful and beautiful? I loved her.

My adopted mother's love for me was magnificent even when she disagreed with me. Yes, once in a blue moon, we may not agree on a particular decision, but we always understand where the other person was coming from. One of the first lessons she taught when I was about to start my college career was, "If you work hard and you are honest, you will go anywhere." She was a very careful woman.

I am also blessed with many friends. Here is one of the faith columns I wrote to honor my friends.

The Blessing of Friendship (published by LNP November 30, 2014)

I vividly remember one of my students jokingly asking me a few years ago if I would be her BFF. "What is BFF?" I asked. She looked at me with amazement, as if I was older than Methuselah, and then she explained, "Best Friends Forever!" Oh, I thought, maybe I am older than Methuselah after all! But the idea of best friends forever brings comfort to me every day, and especially this time of the year!

For this holiday season, I want to share the miracle of friendship with everyone! Of course, there are different types and definitions of friendship, but no matter your definition, enjoy the marvelousness of friendship this season and always! One of the many awesome qualities of God is manifested in friendship through faith.

One of my favorite Bible stories is that of Jonathan and David in first Samuel, Chapter 20. The friendship between Jonathan and David has always fascinated me. I have always thought that the magnet that connected a prince (Jonathan) to a shepherd (David) was beyond the physical appearance. The magnet that connected them was their faith! Jonathan and David were able to look beyond the outward appearance to see the treasure within.

As I was thinking of this topic, the song "What a Friend We Have in Jesus" came to mind. True friendship is more precious than gold and it should always be valued. The one similarity between faith and friendship is that both are made by choice. Faith is a choice, and it begins with a conversation between the individual and God. Friendship is also a choice, and it begins with a conversation between two individuals.

I am blessed with many friends, but I want to share a phrase one of my friends, Tammy, said to me a couple of weeks ago. She said, "We will never change." Tammy is one of the custodians at Millersville University and one of my friends. Tammy is very pleasant and happy. I always look forward to seeing her and getting my hugs. Tammy also told me that seeing me always gives her joy. Tammy and I have never talked outside of our shared workplace, but we treasure our friendship and look forward to seeing each other every day.

Individuals who have good friends from diverse backgrounds are blessed. The foundation of friendship is character; the nature of friendship is service; the motive of friendship is love; and the purpose of friendship is to show our faith in God. What wonderful qualities to possess!

One of the contagious attitudes for making and keeping friends is the right perspective. This means putting more emphasis on real substance and less on the superficial things. Similar to faith, friendship needs both our brain and our heart. We choose to discover and value our faith, the same way we choose to discover and value our friends. Most of us see faith as a gift from God, and do not want to waste that gift. Friendship is also a gift from God.

A quote attributed to the 19th-century evangelist, Dwight Moody reads, "A little faith will bring your soul to heaven, but a lot of faith will bring heaven to your soul."

I have experienced this! In the past, each time I saw pictures of the Grand Canyon, I always thought it was awesome! But when I saw the Grand Canyon in person summer of 2014, I was so overwhelmed with the awesomeness that I fainted. The same is true with friendship. A few friends bring us happiness, but a lot of friends bring splendid happiness to our being! Keep your faith and keep your friends! Happy Holidays!

CHAPTER TEN

BY GOD'S GRACE ALONE

> *For by grace you have been saved*
> *through faith, and that not of yourselves;*
> *it is the gift of God, not of works,*
> *lest anyone should boast.*
> *Ephesians 2: 8-9*

How do you move forward when the injustice, damage, and pain hurt more than you can bear? Of course, I know that the Lord says to "cast all our cares on Him", but I was still struggling with the how to do that. When I started writing faith columns in 2014, most of my thoughts were still on all the mistakes I made, which of course would drag me down emotionally. But as I proceeded with writing these columns, I had no choice but to dig deep in God's word which left me with no time for my self-pity parties.

Raising two boys, full-time job, and studying more in the word of God in preparing for the columns, permeated my thoughts and I started to see clearly…it is not by work of righteousness, but by His grace alone. The heaviness of the emotional baggage started to dissipate, and I was able to see how much God loves me. I also started to see God's hand in everything I went through, and I finally understood what Joseph said in Genesis 50: 20, "But as for you, you meant evil against me; but God meant it for good, in order to bring it about as it is this day, to save many people alive." I want to share a few of the faith columns I wrote with you.

Cleaning for the Soul (published by LNP October 5, 2014)

As someone who loves gardening, fall is one of my favorite seasons. Though fall is the season when most of the beautiful plants and bushes go to sleep, we have faith that the perennials will come back to life in the spring.

This faith added to my love of gardening makes it easy for me to clean the outside of my house, trim the bushes, do the edging and mulching, and see my yard looking beautiful. Fall cleaning inside my house is another story because it is neither fun nor easy for me to do. I could do it if I really, really wanted to, but I just do not enjoy cleaning the inside. Therefore, I convinced myself that it was okay not to clean the inside if I did not like it. In past years, I would pay someone to help me do the major cleaning inside the house.

Then I learned one important lesson from my child last week. (Yes, we can learn from our children too.) This is a beautiful love story.

I gave my 8-year-old son a consequence of five minutes of no talking. For my son, five minutes of no talking is worse than a life sentence to him. My son watched the timer ticking away as he waited for the five minutes to be over, and finally it was. He came and gave me a hug and said, "Mommy, I love you. I just don't like this timer consequence."

As a good parent, I said, "I know that you do not like it, but you were able to do it. How does that make you feel?" He said, "Happy! I did it even though I do not like it."

My son just told me the truth in love!

Yes, five minutes of no talking may seem to be no big deal to many people, but to a child who talks non-stop, that was an injustice. How many things did I not do because I do not like doing them? How many things do most of us not do because we do not like doing them, or because doing those things make us feel uncomfortable?

This reminded me of one difficult and uncomfortable, but important, task I did a while ago: Speaking the truth in love. It was very difficult for me to speak the truth in love until I learned the meaning of forgiveness through faith in God. We live in the world where injustice such as emotional abuse, false accusations, persecution, oppression, (or even five minutes of no talking) happen to innocent people.

Though it is not easy, forgiveness and telling the truth in love would relive us from the bondage of injustice. My son came and gave me a hug and told me that he loves me, but then told me the truth of the injustice I did to him.

Most of us may not have difficulty telling the truth, but truth alone without love is brutal and love alone without truth is hypocrisy.

Refusing to give in to the hatred the injustice caused would strengthen us to tell the truth in love.

Oh, that I may have faith as little as a mustard seed and have the innocence as a child; then telling the truth in love would be easy!

I just finished doing the fall cleaning inside my house. I did not like it, but I did it and like my son I feel happy that I did it. Faith unlocks the door to happiness. It is refreshing to my soul.

Truth plus love equals happiness.

Fasten your belt of truth, it will be a bumpy ride (published by LNP June 25, 2017)

Corrie Ten Boom said, "It is not my ability, but my response to God's ability that counts."

I don't know about you, but I am overwhelmed by the conflicts and chaos that surround us these days, and I need encouragement from the word of God to refocus on the truth about God's ability.

Ephesians 6:13-18 provides us with useful armors of God that we need to help us withstand outside pressures without been crushed when the conflict reaches its fiercest intensity.

God's ability is clearly communicated to us through His word. Life's pressures, such as work, family, health and other concerns can squeeze us until we are spiritually empty. But like David (Psalms 61:2), our spiritual instinct teaches us that we need a rock (God) for protection and guidance.

The first piece of the whole armor of God in Ephesians is the belt of truth. The purpose of belt is to fasten on and hold something together. Therefore, the belt of truth will hold us together and help us focus on God's ability. When we hold on to the truth of God's word, our imaginations would stay focus on God.

It is when we acknowledge that we do not have wisdom or strength to direct our own steps that we rely on God, as our foundation, to help us stand firm in any conflict.

Many people have asked me what I think about the situations unfolding in the country right now. I have always answered, "It does not matter what I think, but what matters is what God says about it." I would further explain that sometimes, God seems to be silent on a given topic, and in such cases, we need to be silent as well. However, when God's word directs us, we should be positive and strong in our faith without wavering.

When the world around me seem hopeless, I turn to the word of God to help me remain strong in the Lord. I drive around different farm sites and think about what farmers see when they stare over open and barren fields. I conclude that the farmers focus on the opportunity, not the rough and rocky grounds. Yes, the work ahead for the farmers is great, but staying focus on the goal help them stay on the right track and move forward.

In like manner, we need to remain steady in the word of God to help us stay focus on what is important. It takes discipline to read the word of God regularly, but the effort is worth it because the Bible remains our source for knowledge about God and about ourselves.

It is not easy to bring every thought into captivity, but as we gird our minds with the belt of truth, our focus will remain on what God is saying to us.

Waiting on the Lord is most important for our growth (published by LNP April 23, 2017)

Psalm 37:7 tells us to "rest in the Lord, and wait patiently for Him."

Waiting is hard for me and waiting patiently is even harder. Many people would agree that waiting is difficult, and it is the thing we do least well, especially when waiting does not seem to release or resolve the situation right away.

How do we rest in the Lord when we are constantly surrounded by the turbulent situations of this world? How long do we need to wait before the Lord steps in and calm the storms?

As I pondered these and other questions, I was reminded of a story I read a while ago. One day, a gardener walked around his garden, and he saw a large and beautiful butterfly. However, the butterfly was fluttering as though in great distress. It seemed to be caught in something that made it difficult to release itself.

The gardener thought it would be a good thing to release the precious thing. Therefore, he took hold of the wings and set it free. The butterfly flew for a few feet and fell to the ground dead.

Under a magnifying glass, the gardener discovered that the butterfly was at the stage of growth, when it was just entering adulthood. Nature fastened to its chrysalis the lifeblood to flow from the tiny arteries of its wings that would allow it to flutter and flutter so that its wings might grow strong. It was the muscle-developing process that nature was giving this young beautiful butterfly.

If only it had only fluttered long enough, the butterfly would have come forth ready for the world. But its premature release ended the beautiful dream.

As we read in the book of Ecclesiastes chapter 3, everything has its time. Though we are not able to see the hidden reason and purpose for why we go through certain circumstances, God knows, and He wants the best for us. God will never prematurely release us from fluttering only to experience destruction.

I do not know how long I need to wait, and I do not know how long you need to wait, before we are ready to be released. But I know that God will make everything beautiful in His time (Ecclesiastes 3:11).

The Lord cares for our every move; therefore, we need to rest in Him. As people of faith, we are privileged to cast all our anxieties on the Lord with confidence that He cares for us.

Isaiah 40:31 states that those who wait on the Lord will renew their strength; they shall mount up with wings like eagles, they shall run and not be weary, they shall walk and not faint.

True faith waits, confident that God is able to do what He has promised us (Romans 4:21).

Waiting is part of the process!

CHAPTER ELEVEN

MY SKIN COLOR IN THE USA

For there is no difference;
For all have sinned and fall short of the glory of God.
Roman 3: 22b-23

Let me tell you three stories relating to my skin color. In 1993, I landed a summer teaching position at a private preschool program before starting at Teachers' College, Columbia University in New York. They were very few light skinned black kids in that school, but no black teacher. Picture a black woman in a white female supervisor's office with the supervisor shaking the black woman's hands. The supervisor wanted to introduce me to the kids, staff, and teachers. Therefore, she took me to different classes. Picture a black woman and a white female supervisor walking and entering a classroom full of kids with one teacher and one teacher assistant who are all white. The kids and the staff stood up and greeted me warmly. I was very happy.

One white girl raised her hand, indicating that she wanted to ask a question. The girl asked me one important question. The girl asked, "Why are you black?" All the grown-up people in that classroom were embarrassed and looked worried. I told all the grown-ups that I had to answer a very important question. I asked the girl if she could help me before I answered her question, and she agreed. I wanted the girl to draw a picture for me first. I gave her a white paper and a white crayon and asked her to draw a picture for me. Then I took a black construction paper and a black crayon and I drew another picture. We both finished our individual pictures. Then I got a yellow construction paper and many colors of crayons and asked her to draw a picture with me on the yellow construction paper. We both drew pictures on the same yellow construction paper using different colors of crayon. Then I asked the girl to pick one picture that she liked best among the three pictures. Can you guess which picture she picked? Yes, she picked the picture on the yellow construction paper. Yeah!!! I asked her why she picked that picture and she said, "Because it is pretty." I said to her, "That is why I am black and you are white. God made you white and me black so that together we can make a beautiful picture." My then three year-old friend said, "Okay" and joined the rest of her group.

The next day, my new friend's mom brought her to school with a gift for us. Her mom brought a chocolate cake with a vanilla icing. My friend's mom said that her daughter asked her a question when she came home a night before. "Mom," my friend asked, "do you know why "Pajama" is black and I am white?" (she could not say my name Ojoma; therefore, she used to call me "Pajama") Her mother was shocked by the question and said, "No." My friend continued, "God made her black and me white, so that together we can make a beautiful picture. Pajama is my friend now." Her mom was very happy about the important lesson that her daughter taught her and she decided to bake a chocolate cake with vanilla icing for us so my three-year old friend and I could eat and celebrate our new friendship. Picture a thirty-three-year-old black woman kneeling on one knee and hugging a pretty blonde Jewish white three-year-old with both of their arms around each other; we were very happy.

God made all of us different so that together we can make a beautiful picture. So that together we can show the love of God. So that together we can accept one another the way God meant it to be. Make a friend today so that together you and your friend can make a beautiful picture.

The next incident provided a different kind of learning experience. I was dating a man who happened to be white. One day we went out to eat, and we pulled into a restaurant parking lot almost at the same time as one other man. This man, whom I will refer to as Bob, was not happy with us for taking the only parking space left, and it was evident that the reason was because we were a "mixed race" couple. He forced my date into a verbal confrontation. However, I told my date to let me fight this one; then I turned to Bob and ask, "Why do you hate black people?" Bob was brave and he decided to tell me everything that was wrong with black people, starting from their laziness to their being dirty. He spewed out a laundry list of reasons why he did not like black people. You can tell that he had practiced this many times. When he finished, I said to him, "I hate them too." I told him that I would not like the black people he described either. I took the "fun" out of this fight for him, so he stood and looked at me strangely.

Something about his look made me ask the next question. I asked, "Do you have children?" He said yes, and proceeded to brag about the two kids he has. He told me that his first born, "Jessica" was attending College to get her degree. He continued by telling me that Jessica is getting her degree in Special Education to help "dumb kids", but Jessica herself is not dumb; but she likes to help them. For some reason, I made a quick connection with one "Jessica Smith" I had in class and I said, "Do you mean Jessica Smith?" He was stunned, but said, "Yes, how do you know her?" I extended my hand out to shake his and said, "My name is Dr. Edeh, I am Jessica's professor."

Well, what happened next cannot be explained in words. His body language and demeanor changed, and you could tell that he wished that the ground on which he was standing would open its mouth and swallow him alive. To his credit, Bob told his daughter of his ignorance and shame. And Jessica came to my class the next time crying and apologizing for her father's behavior. Ignorance is not an excuse for discrimination, but education is one way in which we can change it.

The final experience I want to share is to honor my student's request. By now you may have insight to the relationship I have with my students. I am truly blessed to have great students. Summer of 2006, I was getting read to go home, as usual. When I buy items, clothes, backpacks, etc. to take home, you do not want to see me. I usually buy these items the Saturday before my flight and I always go out to the stores in my Saturday glory!

I went to one store where I could find most of what I needed. When on this mission, I usually do like to talk to people at that moment because I focus on the task at hand. I also used cash because it was easy for me to go over my budget if I did not use cash.

I spent all the $500 budget and I self-checked out. But before I could leave, I was stopped by one of the staff and said, "The store manager needs to check your bags." "Sure", I said, but inside I said, "Here we go again." The white male manager came and asked why I bought so much. I replied, "It is not a crime to buy many items in America." Yes, I was ready for him.

About two minutes into his matching each item to the receipt, my student, oh let me say my white student, let's call her "Sarah" who works there over the summer months saw me from afar and said, "Dr. Edeh, what are you doing here?" She ran towards me and gave me one of the biggest hugs I have ever had. Of course, I never missed opportunity like that, so I said, "Oh, I am stealing merchandise today."

Then she noticed the manager, who was very uncomfortable at that moment. The manager told me that I can leave now, but I said, "No! I am still the same black woman with natural dreads and in her Saturday glory." I told him to go through each item and matched it to the receipt and he did. He told me that he was finished, and I asked how many items I stole, and he said, "None, I'm sorry." I told him not to worry, but he had to pack my bags, folding every item the way I folded it before he came out. At this point, there were a small crowd surrounded us, staff, and customers, and when he bagged my items, I gave my student another hug and left.

One person may not be able to stamped out this deadly disease known as discrimination, but each of us can use our individual styles to call out people who are still stuck in the past.

CHAPTER TWELVE

MATTANIAH = GIFT OF JEHOVAH

*Also that day they offered great sacrifices,
and rejoiced, for God had made them
rejoice with great joy;*
Nehemiah 12: 43a

Fear not, for I am with you;
Be not dismayed, for I am your God.
I will strengthen you, yes,
I will help you, I will uphold you with
My righteous right hand.
Isaiah 41: 10

O magnify the Lord with me,
And let us exalt his name together.
I sought the Lord, and he heard me,
and delivered me from all my fears.
Psalms 34: 3-4

My name Ojoma means "God Knows." God does know what He is doing! I want to use this opportunity to encourage you to put your trust in God and persevere in whatever situation you find yourself. Keep in mind that God knows what He is doing, and we need to trust that. God used many people that I did not know, and never dreamt of knowing, to help me in every way possible because He knows what is best for me.

The Bible tells us that when we ask anything in His Name, while we are in His will believing, He will do it for us. When I finally understood that concept, I started to pray and ask in His will. Every time after that, when I saw myself in a situation, and I felt like all the doors were closing and the walls were caving in on me, I always looked up and each time the Lord airlifted me. No matter what the situation might be, even if you feel like the world has turned against you and all hopes seem lost, look up to the Lord for He will airlift you. Have faith in God and know that when you do not feel like you can hold on, He will never let go of you.

Celebrating mothers and God's wisdom (published by LNP December 23, 2018)

More than one hundred years ago, Ella Wheeler Wilcox published the following short poem:

> *One ship sails East, And another West, By the self-same winds that blow; 'Tis the set of the sails And not the gales That tells the way we go.*

Mothers face storms daily as they protect and raise their children. If they navigate by making godly choices, they will be aligned with the mother described in Proverbs 31, which reads, in part:

> *She sets about her work vigorously; her arms are strong for her tasks. ... She opens her arms to the poor and extends her hands to the needy. ... She is clothed with strength and dignity;*

> *she can laugh at the days to come. She speaks with wisdom, and faithful instruction is on her tongue. She watches over the affairs of her household and does not eat the bread of idleness. Her children arise and call her blessed;*

> *her husband also ... A woman who fears the Lord is to be praised.*

While holding their newborns or cheering for their sons and daughters at sporting activities — whatever task they're undertaking — mothers should look to God for wisdom in raising, providing for, and protecting their children. Mothers' godly choices are rooted in the Bible. For example, Moses' mother, against all odds, hid her son and thereby protected him from the dangerous threat against his life and safety (Exodus 2:2).

Mothers' godly characteristics are found in 2 Timothy 1:7: "God has not given us a spirit of fear, but of power and of love and of a sound mind." With God as the helm, mothers are not afraid of the stormy voyage of raising children. God has given us the spirit of power. Through the Holy Spirit, mothers stand firm with inner spiritual strength to serve their families with patience, to overcome obstacles.

God has given us the spirit of love. The love that mothers have for their children is one of the strongest of all human emotions. When we become mothers, we become partners with God and we take this partnership seriously. Both the Bible and the commercial world agree that the core Christmas message is one of giving fueled by love. To love is a duty, consistent with the character of God, and no one takes this duty more seriously than mothers.

Legend has it that St. Nicholas (or Santa Claus) was a generous monk who gave all he owned away to help the poor and the sick. For many years, St. Nicholas became known for his gift-giving, especially on Christmas Eve.

In the Bible, we read that God so loved the world that he gave his only begotten Son (John 3:16).

One of the qualities that makes love unique is that it acts without expectation of getting something in return. Mothers work their fingers to the bone and even if their children do not rise up and call them blessed, as in Proverb 31, mothers would never stop loving them.

Though mothers wear many hats and work both inside and outside the home, God gives mothers the spirit of a sound mind — the spirit of self-control to maintain balanced judgement in our dealings with our children and others.

Mothers, may we continue to live a godly legacy for our children, for one day they will rise up and call us blessed. Merry Christmas!

In conclusion, I want to share a portion of the article written by Ed Fleming for The Lancaster Patriot, published the week of May 16th thru May 23rd, 2022.

A Ministry of Hope Helps Individuals with Intellectual Disabilities Function in Society

Very soon the sound of "Pomp and Circumstance" will be echoing across the USA as schools bid farewell to another class of graduating seniors. Thirteen years, from Kindergarten to High School of instruction and training will have been completed by students. The graduates from high schools would go their different ways to pursue their unique paths to obtain the "American Dream." Some of the high school graduates would further their education via a four college or trade school while other graduates choose to go into the workforce right out of high school. However, the paths to obtain the American Dream for the high school graduates with intellectual disabilities and/or autism are not as straightforward or clear as their peers without such challenges.

These struggles must be addressed so that people with intellectual disabilities can operate more successfully in a society that requires certain cognitive capabilities – and Olive Branch of Hope offers solution. The organization was founded in May 2014 by Ojoma Edeh Herr, who holds a doctorate degree in special education. Herr wanted to find a way to help individual with intellectual disabilities thrive, and Olive Branch of Hope is her way of sharing the opportunity.

Located in the scenic, historic city of Lancaster, Olive Branch of Hope offers a community-integrated program, providing adults, eighteen years and up, who have autism and intellectual disabilities. The program is built around giving participants opportunities to improve their social skills and learn how to live independently. Daily living skills, self-expression, and other useful skills are taught through experiences such as outdoor adventures, working with animals, summer camps and arts, with each activity taking into account the individuals interests. This non-traditional approach to learning requires individuals with intellectual disabilities' input in the activities. The process allows for incorporation and infusion of individuals' diverse interests into the activities and materials to help them acquire the strategies they need to be successful in their communities, homes and in life; thereby become productive members of the society. Participants learn effective problem-solving strategies through interest based.

"Everyone deserves opportunity to obtain the American Dream, Herr told The Lancaster Patriot. "The major goal of Olive Branch of Hope is to assist individuals with intellectual disabilities in acquiring, maintaining, and improving self-help, domestic, socialization, and adaptive skills necessary to reside successfully in their homes and communities."

"The USA and Lancaster have helped me in fulfilling my dreams, so the least I can do is give back," she said.

She has been able to push forward against the odds and accomplish a great deal, and she attributes her perseverance and achievements to her faith. "Here are a few of my memory verses: Isaiah 41:10, 'Fear not, for I am with you; be not dismayed for I am your God. I will strengthen you, yes, I will help you, I will uphold you with My righteous right hand.' Psalm 27:1, 'The Lord is salvation, whom shall, I fear? The Lord is the strength of my life, of whom shall I be afraid?' I am a child of the living God; therefore, I truly should not be afraid to serve, using my education."

All I need is faith as little as a mustard seed and the Lord would show Himself.

www.ingramcontent.com/pod-product-compliance
Lightning Source LLC
LaVergne TN
LVHW041225080526
838199LV00083B/3309